Portfolio Development for Preservice Teachers

by
Diane Hood Nettles
and
Pamela Bondi Petrick

Library of Congress Catalog Card Number 95-67073
ISBN 0-87367-379-4

This fastback is sponsored by the six chapters in Area 5C (Wisconsin) of Phi Delta Kappa. These chapters made a generous contribution toward publication costs. The chapters in Area 5C are:

University of Wisconsin/Madison
Marquette University
Milwaukee
Whitewater Wisconsin
Kenosha-Racine Wisconsin
Lake Country Wisconsin Area

Table of Contents

Introduction

e afternoon, after a faculty meeting at our small state university, ɔers of the elementary education faculty were chatting about their nts' job-hunting efforts. One professor recounted her recent visit ocal school and a conversation with a principal. This principal ɔld her about needing to fill four teaching positions. He had re- d more than 800 applications.

ar faculty member asked him, "What made the difference in your ion of whom to hire?"

ɪe principal had begun with a thorough examination of the appli- transcripts, which resulted in the initial interview pool. Then the ipal talked about the candidates' self-confidence and enthusiasm interview, their knowledge of content and pedagogy, and a va- of other factors. But one factor stood out from all the others. All ɛ teachers he hired had come to the interview with a profession- tfolio.

hat," he said, "really impressed me."

ɪr several months, members of our faculty had been kicking around for assessing and evaluating our students in more holistic ways. ɪd become concerned that a mixed message was being sent to our nts. As advocates of such teaching philosophies as whole lan- ɛ, we were encouraging our own preservice teachers to become ɪatchers" (Goodman 1986) and to continually examine all facets rning that add to the child's whole being. Yet we were focusing ades as the only measure of a preservice teacher's ability, and

7

many of us had no idea of what our students were capable of doing beyond the activities that were done in our own classes. As one of faculty remarked, "I never have the opportunity to see the whole picture of our students' abilities, because the only product I ever see is grade I've given them!"

That comment turned the conversation toward departmental evaluation. How could we assess our effectiveness as teacher educators? Some of the methods we had used in the past were exit interviews, on the number of our graduates who found employment, surveys of graduates' employers, and observations of our students as student teachers. However, these are summative methods that focus on products, just as grades do. We were interested in formative evaluation so that we could evaluate ourselves *and* our preservice teachers as progressed through our teacher education program.

It became clear to us that we needed to develop methods of assessment and self-evaluation that would reflect more accurately the learning processes of our students. Such assessment also would reflect goals more accurately, and we would be better able to document when we reached our goals by using a more holistic method of assessment. As "facilitators of learning" for our preservice education students (Campbell 1990, p. 8), we felt that we needed to be more diagnostic and self-reflective in the evaluation of our student's abilities. At the same time, we wanted our students to gain more control over their learning by doing the same thing.

The climate was right for moving away from reliance on traditional assessment methods toward a broader, more flexible approach. the concept of portfolio assessments for our preservice teachers born.

Our approach addressed two specific questions:

1. Have we met our goals as teachers? The answer to this question would help us to evaluate ourselves as individual teachers as a department.

Have students met the learning goals established for the teacher education program? The answer to this question would help students evaluate themselves, in addition to allowing the faculty to evaluate students.

cause portfolios are personal collections of "materials that re-
rogress toward intended learning goals" (Ryan and Kuhs 1993,
, we believed that the development of portfolios would help us
r these questions.

is fastback describes the process that we undertook to begin us-
rtfolios in our elementary teacher training program. First, we
y define the concept of portfolios and provide a rationale for their
teacher education programs. Then we describe the portfolio
ss, including a detailed description of the six steps involved in
ing portfolios for documenting professional growth in a teacher
tion program. We show how program goals, or outcomes, serve
undation for the construction of portfolios.

Concept and Rationale

For many years artists have documented their work using colle of authentic samples of their artistic expression. Our memories of ing across a campus during our own college years include visic student artists toting black, cumbersome, poster-size folders in a of elevators, dorms, and classrooms. When we glimpsed into the ers of our artist friends, we found not only collections of polished but also curious and idiosyncratic works that conveyed a sense artist's diversity of thoughts and pursuits in the field of art. Thes ollections of the artists' portfolios gave us a foundation for our tho about portfolios in general.

Preservice education portfolios are collections of authentic, le specific documents that give evidence of growth and developme ward becoming teachers. Portfolios also are an acknowledgmen teacher development is an individualized process. They reflect dent's progress over time and, just as important, they help to docu whether we on the faculty are succeeding in meeting our goa preparing teachers.

We specifically use portfolios in three ways:

To evaluate the preservice teacher education program. As stu begin to create portfolios, patterns evolve. We begin to see tha dents are able to document some skills and abilities better than o This provides us with opportunities to improve our courses, as ments, and syllabi.

• *enhance and document active student learning.* Portfolios help ᴫvice teachers become more active in their own learning. Because folio is self-initiated documentation of growth, students select items included. This gives them control over their own learning, aware- ᴐf their own strengths and weaknesses, and the opportunity to make es about how they wish to present themselves as professionals.

• *provide students with a personal marketing tool after gradua-* Portfolios provide evidence of teaching skills, achievements, and ies for prospective employers. They are more reflective of per- strengths and are more revealing about the preservice teacher a transcript or test score.

The Portfolio Process

There are six steps in initiating the portfolio process for prese teacher education. Faculty should:

1. Adopt a philosophy statement.
2. Decide on outcomes that reflect the teacher education prog
3. Decide the purpose(s) for using portfolios in the program.
4. Select specific types of artifacts — such as reports, work ples, etc. — that students will include to document outcon
5. Decide a process for implementing portfolios.
6. Write a manual to serve as a guide for faculty and student:

Step One: Adopt a Philosophy Statement

In the process of our program review, we concluded that our tea reflected one basic theory of learning. Our goal for teaching pr vice teachers is to provide them with an orientation to a develop tal interactionist view to teaching and learning (Biber 1976; Cam 1990). This view posits that children learn by constructing their knowledge based on their environment, with the teacher acting as cilitator rather than as a dispenser of knowledge. Thus we adopte statement as our departmental philosophy.

For departments and schools to effectively implement the u portfolios, we recommend that a similar discussion take place. Fa need to reach consensus about the learning theories that guide and shape the teacher education program. Putting this consensus

le, succinct philosophy statement makes an effective starting point
e development of the portfolio program.

Two: Decide on Outcomes

ased on our philosophy statement, we decided on outcomes that
ted the program. These outcomes were specific behaviors that
eemed to be necessary for good teaching to occur.

e use of outcomes is vital because they are the goals toward which
ation faculty and students will work. They are the statements that
the building of a professional portfolio. The number of outcomes
ded in the program is not as important as their comprehensiveness,
reflection on what the faculty believes is important for teachers
ow and do, and their adherence to the philosophy of the educa-
department or college.

1990 our department had written a set of student outcomes that
then revised in 1993. The revision was based on the principles
ed in September 1992 by the Interstate New Teacher Assessment
Support Consortium, a division of the Council of Chief State
ol Officers. The principles from the INTASC were chosen for two
ns. First, they reflected what we believe about teaching and learn-
Second, they are part of a sound plan for national licensing of
ers. We felt that it was important for our outcomes to reflect both
ese factors. Our interpretation of the INTASC principles evolved
10 outcome statements that reflect areas of personal and profes-
l development. Following are those 10 statements:

utcome 1: Formal and informal assessment skills. Preservice
ers should have not only a knowledge of assessment strategies
lso the ability to use this information for the positive development
eir students. A wide variety of assessment methods, both formal
nformal, will help preservice teachers become more aware of their
nts' attitudes and interests, as well as their academic develop-
. While formal assessments, such as achievement and aptitude

13

tests, yield readily identifiable scores, they do not cover all of the
that are taught. Informal assessments, on the other hand, can tes
skill that is taught and so alert the teacher to weak areas for ⟨
remediation.

It is important for preservice teachers to realize that there are ⟩
ways of demonstrating their skills in assessing students. Many pr
vice teachers associate assessment with traditional number scores,
as those derived from standardized achievement tests or aptitude
However, informal reading inventories, anecdotal records, infc
observations, checklists, informal interviews, interest inventories,
ing samples, questionnaires, metacognition surveys, and portfoli⟨
qualify as assessment tools. All of these are possible artifact
documentation.

Outcome 2: Diagnosis and matchmaking skills. Using educati
social, cultural, and psychological data, preservice teachers shou
able to implement learning experiences that are appropriate for tl
dividuals and groups observed. Although preservice teachers co
the classroom with their own beliefs about how children learn, it i
portant that they now make sound judgments about which instruct
strategies to use, modify, or reject according to the needs of their
ent classroom. Observation will help verify students' strengths, w
nesses, knowledge, and skills, which will be necessary in plann
successful program. Practice in observation will sharpen prese
teachers' ability to identify the optimal match between the student
their educational, social, and cultural experiences.

Artifacts that might provide documentation of this outcome in⟨
reflective journals, lessons and unit plans, critiques of lessons,
vidualized plans and contracts, and observation reports.

Outcome 3: Knowledge and use of environments and materia
this outcome is met, the preservice teacher becomes a facilitat
learning who helps children construct their own knowledge by
nipulating materials, interacting with new information, and enga

14

aningful experiences with peers. Preservice teachers must have
ility to create responsive environments for learning with a wide
y of interesting materials in a flexible and functional classroom
gement. In addition, preservice teachers need to recognize that
tive and affective objectives are integrated in all areas of the cur-
m. Preservice teachers might document their understandings in
rea by including activities in their portfolios that reflect discovery
ing, inquiry learning, problem solving, inductive learning, child-
ted learning, social collaboration, and play as a learning medium.
tifacts that might qualify under this outcome include floor plans,
s of creative teaching materials, lesson plans, examples of col-
ative planning, examples of student products, integrated unit plans,
a competency checklists, plans for child-initiated learning, jour-
tries, and supervisor evaluations.

tcome 4: Instructional planning skills. This outcome acknowl-
 that teachers are able to use a variety of teaching strategies that
 rage students' development of critical thinking, problem solving,
 ecision making. Instruction may involve the use of simulations,
 nstrations, cooperative learning, role playing, experimentation
 discovery, anticipation guides, mapping, analogies, and student
 ioning. Therefore, effective thinking is both creative and critical.
 sson plans are the most helpful artifact for documenting this out-
 . Specific teaching strategies might be highlighted in various
 .

tcome 5: Classroom management skills. Facilitating positive so-
 teraction, active engagement in learning, and self-motivation are
 rtant goals for the preservice teacher. To reach these goals, the pre-
 e teacher should know how to provide and maintain a classroom
 onment that is conducive to learning without inhibiting personal
 th and group cooperation. Intrinsic motivation, rather than exter-
 wards and punishments, becomes possible because learning is rel-
 , meaningful, challenging, and developmentally appropriate.

Artifact possibilities include classroom rules and procedures, c
erative learning strategies, daily classroom schedules, and a disci
philosophy.

Outcome 6: Knowledge of philosophical and social influe
Preservice teachers should be able to plan instruction effectively.
planning reflects their knowledge of subject matter, but it also inv
much more. Plans must be made within a philosophical frame
one that the preservice teacher has chosen independently. The r
of the students that they will teach must be part of this philoso
framework, so that the students' cognitive, affective, and ph
growth will be facilitated. In addition, the needs of the community
be considered, because students interact with the world outsid
classroom. Parent and community standards and expectations mu
considered. Without such an orientation, the teacher risks mere
cusing on filling time with activities, rather than offering a col
program that has purpose. Our responsibility as teacher educator
introduce philosophical orientations from which preservice tea
can make both long-term and short-term plans.

Preservice teachers might document their abilities to plan instru
that takes into account philosophical and social influences by using
types of artifacts, including correspondence with community resou
lesson or unit plans in which philosophical beliefs are evident and
lighted, personal mission or philosophy statements, position pape
flective journal entries, and letters to parents.

Outcome 7: Knowledge of content. The central concepts, tools
quiry, and structures of the content areas taught at the early child
and elementary levels are essential for preservice teachers. Beca
the diverse nature of elementary school teaching, it is important fo
service teachers to be well-versed in all subjects that young childr
taught. Such a knowledge must encompass the ability to create l
ing experiences that make the subject matter meaningful to chi
Thus preservice teachers must be facilitators of knowledge in

. This outcome is twofold: First, the teacher must know the sub-
ᵥell. Second, the teacher must know how to teach the subject well.
ssible artifacts for documenting this outcome are lesson plans,
rch papers, National Teachers' Exam (NTE) scores, subject matter
, and critiques of video scenarios.

utcome 8: Knowledge of child development. It is important for the
rvice teacher to know how children and adolescents learn and de-
. This knowledge sets them apart from mere dispensers of knowl-
. Their abilities to provide learning opportunities are influenced
eir knowledge of the intellectual, social/emotional, and physical
lopment of their young students. Thus children and pre-adoles-
can learn in an environment that is conducive to their growth and
being.

rtifact possibilities include anecdotal records; student assess-
s; case studies of students; examples of individualized lesson plans
ns adapted for special learners; interviews with students, parents,
achers; and portfolio entries provided by children.

utcome 9: Professional commitment and responsibility. Self-re-
ion is the mark of a good teacher. The preservice teacher should
ate continually the effects of his or her choices and actions on
ren, parents, and other professionals. This type of evaluation is
red when the preservice teacher seeks ways to continue learning
de the college classroom, such as through active membership in
essional societies, attendance at workshops, and community work.
actions help the preservice teacher to evaluate what he or she
ws" and to modify previously held ideas about teaching. Greater
essional growth is the result.

here are many ways to document professional commitment and
nsibility. Some artifacts are correspondence with community re-
ces, logs of professional meetings and workshops, evidence of
al subscriptions, summaries of volunteer experiences, and evi-
e of professional organization or committee memberships.

Outcome 10: School-home-community cooperation. One of the important facets of teaching lies outside the classroom. Indeed, th rounding community may have more influence over students than school. The preservice teacher who is aware of this makes good ι community resources, at the same time serving as a resource ι community. The ability to work well with parents and social age is essential to the cooperative effort needed in educating childre addition, preservice teachers need to seek opportunities to enhance awareness of the cultural environment in the community.

The following artifacts might be used to document proficien this outcome statement: evidence of community involvement, e ples of collaborative planning, letters of recommendation from munity leaders, critiques of cultural events, and pictures from par meetings or workshops.

Step Three: Decide the Purpose for Portfolios

In determining the advantages of a portfolio system in our prog five reasons for using them evolved:

1. Portfolios allow preservice teachers to organize their work
2. Portfolios require that preservice teachers rationalize the portance of their documents.
3. Portfolios require preservice teachers to reflect on their work.
4. Portfolios help preservice teachers to see a purpose for their lege assignments in the education program.
5. Portfolios require professors of education to reflect on their work.

Each of these reasons merits further explanation. First, prese teachers begin to organize their work by building a portfolio. W we suggest several types of artifacts for each outcome category preservice teachers have the freedom to choose the documents

to include. Categorizing artifacts that reflect program outcomes
s them to see the types of abilities they are developing as they
lete their education courses. Strengths as well as weaknesses be-
evident.

aturally, the quality of some artifacts will be better than others,
g preservice teachers a picture of the challenges that lay before
. For example, on examining the contents of her working port-
a preservice teacher may realize that she is quite good at writing
ion papers that reflect her beliefs, but her abilities to write lesson
are not as strong. This insight gives her a goal toward which to

cond, preservice teachers must provide a rationale for their choice
cuments. Each artifact is accompanied by a required rationale
. The rationale is a statement explaining the reason for inserting
rtifact into the chosen outcome category. Writing a rationale al-
our students to reflect on their work, both in deciding for which
me the artifact provides evidence and in realizing their profi-
y in that particular teaching skill. According to Cole (1992), the
nale statements are as important as the artifacts themselves:

> Artifacts have little meaning, however, without reflections. By pro-
> ding both the artifacts and the reflections, an authentic and multi-
> tured view of actual teaching that took place as well as the insight
> to the thinking behind the teaching occur. (p. 10)

hird, preservice teachers reflect on their own work. Including the
nale page for each artifact means that preservice teachers must
the skill of reflective writing. Because they tend to summarize
r than analyze (Cole 1992; Van Mannen 1977), many preservice
ers need training in this skill. Such training is necessary for more
fulfilling the portfolio requirements. A good teacher is able to re-
on and analyze his or her instructional decisions, the students'
ucts, and the learning climate. This type of reflection leads to pro-
onal growth. Reflection might take place merely in one's head dur-

ing idle hours; however, the ability to write reflectively in a col
manner so that others can understand the reflection and perhaps
efit from it is one of the responsibilities of a true professional.

Fourth, preservice teachers should see a purpose for their as
ments in the college of education. Often students complain that as
ments are mere "busy work," and so they complete them grudg
and without commitment. However, once assignments are inclu
artifacts in the outcome categories, preservice teachers begin t
that they are indeed working toward real and specific goals.

Some outcomes are documented more easily than others. Th
flects our program and causes us to look at the types of assignr
that we give to our students. It may become necessary to allow
freedom of choices in assignments. For instance, a student migl
amine his working portfolio and discover that he has no documer
Outcome 6 (knowledge of philosophical and social influences). F
reading methods class, his professor has given an assignment t
tique a professional journal article on the subject of reading. Allc
this student a wider choice of articles will enable him to documer
outcome more effectively. For example, the student might read a
ticle that discusses philosophical points of view and how they a
fluenced by society and then analyze it in terms of what this mea
the reading teacher. Thus the portfolio might allow a student to
more control over his or her learning while still meeting our de
mental goals.

Fifth, the portfolio is a means of self-evaluation for our depart
We challenge our students to look for undocumented outc
throughout their coursework. It becomes our challenge as well to
sure our program is doing what we intend it to do. If we find tha
come statements are not well-documented by several of our stuc
then this finding means that we need to teach more carefully to
that outcome and provide more opportunities for practicing those s
After all, the outcome statements are our goals. We want to be su
are doing what we can to help our students meet them.

Four: Select Types of Artifacts

a department, we brainstormed a variety of artifacts that would propriate evidence for these student outcomes. Ideas came from room assignments that we have given to our students, as well as reference letters, teacher evaluations, transcripts, and résumés, students already were gathering. We gave some thought to the bility of categorizing the artifacts for the students and making a artifacts that could be used for each outcome statement. However, of our goals was to enable our students to exert more control over own learning. Therefore, we simply listed the possible artifacts glossary in our manual, titled "Portfolio Development Manual" pbell et al. 1993). The glossary defines what we mean by the in-ual artifact terms and makes suggestions for the types of skills each artifact may document. The preservice teachers decide for selves where to place their artifacts in their portfolios.

llowing are a few of the possible artifacts:

anecdotal records	literature logs
article summaries	observation reports
bulletin board ideas	peer critiques
computer programs	position papers
copies of awards	reflective journals
discipline philosophy	sample parent letters
lesson plans	supervisor's evaluations

glossary entry is provided for each possible artifact. Following ample entry:

Lesson plans — Copies of your lesson plans should include all com-nents of a workable plan: objectives, materials, introduction, proce-res, closing and evaluation. Sometimes plans may be used for more an one outcome. In this case, highlight the specific part of the plan at documents the outcome. Instructional planning skills will be most viously documented with lesson plans; however, it is possible that owledge of content, use of environments and materials, and knowl-

edge of child development could be documented here. (Campbell et
1993, p. 22)

Step Five: Describe the Process for Implementing Portfolios

Building a portfolio is a process, leading to a product. Prese
teachers begin their teacher education program with a working
folio, which documents growth throughout their academic caree
their education progresses, they make decisions about which c
ments to include in the portfolio. Portfolios are not meant to be
scriptive and restrictive" (Ryan and Kuhs 1993, p. 79), but rather
ible documentation of growth. As time passes, preservice tea
choose to exclude some documents and add new ones, docume
the fact that learning takes place through mistakes and reflectic
those mistakes. Conscious decisions by preservice teachers are e
plified in the process of building a portfolio, because they select
tify, and show their best work, their philosophies, their priorities
their perspectives on the profession. Thus students in the educ
program are in control of their own portfolios.

As they near graduation, students complete the process by cre
a final product, the presentation portfolio. At this point, student
encouraged to include only a few specific documents. Employe
not have time to examine portfolios for longer than about five min
Principals in particular are interested in a prospective teacher's
folio, but they want to see only the most pertinent information (Sn
and Newman 1992). Therefore, we recommend that students b
lective in what they choose for the presentation portfolio. No more
one or two quality documents in each section are needed. In addi
we recommend that students include the following items:

- Résumé
- Three letters of recommendation
- Student teaching evaluations

Philosophy of education statement
Lesson plans that specifically address outcomes
Autobiography

order to gain the advantages of using the portfolio, careful guide-
need to be followed. We decided that five checkpoints needed to
de during the preservice teacher's college career. At each of these
points, the preservice teacher confers with an advisor about the
ess of the working portfolio. The five checkpoints occur: 1) during
rst professional education course that the student takes, 2) during
aluation and measurements course, 3) on completion of 12 credit
in the teacher education program, 4) during the admission to the
nt teaching screening process, and 5) on completion of student
ing, at which point the working portfolio is refined to become a
ntation portfolio.

e following sequence of portfolio development has worked well
:

On enrolling in the entry level curriculum class as a sophomore,
students obtain and read the "Portfolio Development Manual"
written by our department members (Campbell et al. 1993).

Students purchase a notebook and enough tabs to index each outcome listed in the manual.

Students are asked to examine the possible artifacts that are de-
scribed in the manual and become familiar with the types of artifacts that can be used to document the outcomes.

Students begin to collect artifacts and tentatively place them
within an outcome category.

For each artifact, students write a rationale statement that ex-
plains why the artifact was chosen for that outcome statement.
In addition, they describe how this artifact enabled them to grow
in this teaching skill. As time goes on, some artifacts may need
to be rearranged under a different outcome.

6. At the end of the curriculum course, the student meets wi
   professor for a portfolio interview. During this interview
   discuss the student's progress toward goals and understa
   of the portfolio process. Quality, rather than quantity, of
   ments and rationale statements is most important.
7. On enrollment in the tests and measurements course, stu
   prepare to share the portfolio with the professor in an inte
8. As their coursework progresses, students continue to collec
   facts and write rationale statements, concentrating on outcome
   are not yet well-documented. They find ways to document
   including asking their professors for guidance in helping to
   assignments meet goals. By this point, they may find it eas
   place artifacts under the most appropriate outcome statem
9. After completing 12 credit hours in the teacher educatio
   gram, the advisors interview their students, who are ask
   bring their portfolio to the interview, show their docum
   progress, and explain their goals.
10. Students continue to document outcomes throughout their co
    work. By the time they are ready to apply for admission t
    dent teaching, they should have most outcomes documente
    this point, they prepare for another interview with their fa
    advisor about the portfolio. Outcomes that are not well-
    mented are examined as possible areas of challenge for st
    teaching. Strengths are discussed, and the students make
    to capitalize on these strengths during student teaching.
11. When the student teaching term is complete, the student's
    ing portfolio is ready to become a presentation portfolio.
    helps the preservice teachers become marketable when the
    ply for teaching positions.

Step Six: Write a Manual

In order to facilitate our students' understanding of the proce
portfolio development, we developed the manual to which we ha

. This manual is designed to provide flexible guidance in helping
its to build their portfolios. All students are required to purchase
anual when they enroll in their first curriculum and methods
at the end of their sophomore year. The manual contains four

finition of Portfolios
idelines for Assembling
tcome Statements
ssary of Artifacts

iile writing the manual for our preservice teachers, we tried to
pate some questions they might have as they developed their port-
and included responses to such questions as:

iat is the difference between a working portfolio and a presentation portfolio?
hat type of notebook should I use?
hat should I do to the inside of the notebook?
w do I document outcomes?
w do I create a presentation portfolio?
w do I make my presentation portfolio unique?

Conclusion

It has been almost two years since that faculty meeting when ou discussion of preservice teacher portfolios occurred. As a result plementation, we are experiencing a heightened awareness of the for portfolios in our program. Our students actually seem reliev have a tangible piece of evidence that shows they are indeed gro and learning. Many students see the portfolio as a chance to sho their progress, and they are proud of their own expertise.

Portfolios also have created a bridge between students and fa because we are both working to complete common goals. Faculty had the opportunity to re-examine our program. Students' comr concerning the "holes" in their outcome documentation cause us to more closely at the assignments we give to them and the outcome we expect them to have upon graduation.

This approach to implementing portfolio development in a te: education program has worked for us. It outlined the underlying pl ophy of our department, it specified measurable outcomes desi for preservice teachers, it suggested possibilities for documenting outcomes, and it delineated a timetable for implementation. In tion, it dealt with questions that preservice teachers ask on their to developing their own marketability as professionals.

By following this approach, other teacher education departn may find, as we have found, that portfolio development sparks e siastic interest in both faculty and students. The process has ener us to continue our best efforts in facilitating the professional gr of our future teachers.

References

B. "The Developmental-Interactor Point of View." In *The Preschool in
ion, 2nd ed., edited by M.C. Day and R.K. Parker. Boston: Allyn and
:on, 1976.

)ell, D. A Model of the Elementary/Early Childhood Program."
.nuscript, California University of Pennsylvania, California, Pa., 1990.

)ell, D.; Melenyzer, B.; Nettles, D.; Petrick, P.; and Wyman, R. "Portfolio
velopment: A Manual for Preservice Teachers." Manuscript, California
iversity of Pennsylvania, California, Pa., 1993.

D.J. "The Developing Professional: Process and Product Portfolios."
ler presented at the annual meeting of the American Association of
lleges for Teacher Education, San Antonio, 1992. ERIC Document
production Service No. ED 342 731.

nan, K. *What's Whole in Whole Language.* Portsmouth, N.H.:
inemann, 1986.

:ate New Teacher Assessment and Support Consortium. *Model Standards
Beginning Teachers Licensing and Development: A Resource for State
alogue.* Washington, D.C.: Council of Chief State School Officers, 1992.

J.M., and Kuhs, T.M. "Assessments of Preservice Teachers and the Use
Portfolios." *Theory into Practice* 32 (Spring 1993): 75-81.

n, L., and Newman, C. "Portfolios: An Estimate of Their Validity and
icticality." Paper presented at the Annual Meeting of the Eastern
ucational Research Association, Hilton Head, S.C., March 1992. ERIC
cument Reproduction Service No. ED 342 820.

annen, M. "Linking Ways of Knowing with Ways of Being Practical."
rriculum Inquiry* 6 (November 1977): 205-28.

Phi Delta Kappa Fastbacks

wo annual series, published each spring and fall,
r fastbacks on a wide range of educational topics.
1 fastback is intended to be a focused, authoritative
tment of a topic of current interest to educators
other readers. Several hundred fastbacks have
1 published since the program began in 1972,
1y of which are still in print. Among the topics are:

ninistration	Mainstreaming
ılt Education	Multiculturalism
Arts	Nutrition
Risk Students	Parent Involvement
eers	School Choice
sorship	School Safety
nunity Involvement	Special Education
nputers	Staff Development
riculum	Teacher Training
ision Making	Teaching Methods
pout Prevention	Urban Education
eign Study	Values
ed and Talented	Vocational Education
al Issues	Writing

or a current listing of available fastbacks and other
lications of the Educational Foundation, please
tact Phi Delta Kappa, 408 N. Union, P.O. Box 789,
omington, IN 47402-0789, or (812) 339-1156.

Phi Delta Kappa Educational Foundat

The Phi Delta Kappa Educational Foundation
established on 13 October 1966 with the signing, by
George H. Reavis, of the irrevocable trust agreen
creating the Phi Delta Kappa Educational Founda
Trust.

George H. Reavis (1883-1970) entered the educa
profession after graduating from Warrensb
Missouri State Teachers College in 1906 and the U
versity of Missouri in 1911. He went on to earn
M.A. and a Ph.D. at Columbia University. Dr. Re
served as assistant superintendent of schools
Maryland and dean of the College of Arts and Scier
and the School of Education at the University
Pittsburgh. In 1929 he was appointed director of
struction for the Ohio State Department of Educat
But it was as assistant superintendent for curricul
and instruction in the Cincinnati public schools (1￲
48) that he rose to national prominence.

Dr. Reavis' dream for the Educational Founda
was to make it possible for seasoned educators
write and publish the wisdom they had acquired c
a lifetime of professional activity. He wanted edu
tors and the general public to "better understand
the nature of the educative process and (2) the rela
of education to human welfare."

The Phi Delta Kappa fastbacks were begun in 1￲
These publications, along with monographs and bo
on a wide range of topics related to education, are
realization of that dream.